Immortal Invisible

Hymn Settings for
2 Violins with Piano Accompaniment

Kristin Campbell

Download demo recordings, practice tracks, accompaniment tracks, and a pdf file of the violin parts at:

https://horsehairmusic.com/immortal-invisible/10012024

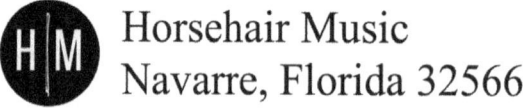 Horsehair Music
Navarre, Florida 32566

Print ISBN: 978-1-959514-21-3
ebook ISBN: 978-1-959514-22-0

Table of Contents

This Is My Father's World

TERRA BETA
Franklin Shepherd
Arr. KRISTIN CAMPBELL (ASCAP)

THIS IS MY FATHER'S WORLD - 2

THIS IS MY FATHER'S WORLD - 3

THIS IS MY FATHER'S WORLD - 5

Be Still My Soul

FINLANDIA
Jean Sibelius
Arr. KRISTIN CAMPBELL (ASCAP)

BE STILL MY SOUL - 4

Immortal, Invisible God Only Wise

ST. DENIO
Welsh Hymn Tune
Arr. KRISTIN CAMPBELL (ASCAP)

IMMORTAL, INVISIBLE GOD ONLY WISE - 3

IMMORTAL, INVISIBLE GOD ONLY WISE - 5

Christ Arose (Lo in the Grave He Lay)

CHRIST AROSE
Robert Lowery
Arr. KRISTIN CAMPBELL (ASCAP)

CHRIST AROSE - 2

CHRIST AROSE - 4

Like A River Glorious

WYE VALLEY
James Mountain
Arr. KRISTIN CAMPBELL (ASCAP)

LIKE A RIVER GLORIOUS - 2

LIKE A RIVER GLORIOUS - 3

LIKE A RIVER GLORIOUS - 4

28

LIKE A RIVER GLORIOUS - 5

LIKE A RIVER GLORIOUS - 7

Rock of Ages

TOPLADY
Thomas Hastings
Arr. KRISTIN CAMPBELL (ASCAP)

ROCK OF AGES - 3

ROCK OF AGES - 4

Guide Me O Thou Great Jehovah

Apples in Winter (Jig)

CWM RHONDDA
John Hughes
Arr. KRISTIN CAMPBELL (ASCAP)

GUIDE ME O THOU GREAT JEHOVAH - 2

GUIDE ME O THOU GREAT JEHOVAH - 4

GUIDE ME O THOU GREAT JEHOVAH - 6

N

Hark the Herald Angels Sing

MENDELSSOHN
Felix Mendelssohn
Arr. KRISTIN CAMPBELL (ASCAP)

HARK THE HERALD ANGELS SING - 3

HARK THE HERALD ANGELS SING - 5

* Small notes and 8va optional

HARK THE HERALD ANGELS SING - 7

The Love of God

LOVE OF GOD
F. M. Lehman
Arr. KRISTIN CAMPBELL (ASCAP)

THE LOVE OF GOD - 2

THE LOVE OF GOD - 4

Sleepers Awake

WACHET AUF
J.S. Bach
Arr. KRISTIN CAMPBELL (ASCAP)

SLEEPERS AWAKE - 3

SLEEPERS AWAKE - 5

SLEEPERS AWAKE - 7

This Is My Father's World

VIOLIN I

TERRA BETA
Franklin Shepherd
Arr. KRISTIN CAMPBELL (ASCAP)

VIOLIN II

This Is My Father's World

TERRA BETA
Franklin Shepherd
Arr. KRISTIN CAMPBELL (ASCAP)

VIOLIN I

Be Still My Soul

FINLANDIA
Jean Sibelius
Arr. KRISTIN CAMPBELL (ASCAP)

VIOLIN II

Be Still My Soul

FINLANDIA
Jean Sibelius
Arr. KRISTIN CAMPBELL (ASCAP)

66

VIOLIN I

Immortal, Invisible God Only Wise

ST. DENIO
Welsh Hymn Tune
Arr. KRISTIN CAMPBELL (ASCAP)

Immortal, Invisible God Only Wise

VIOLIN II

ST. DENIO
Welsh Hymn Tune
Arr. KRISTIN CAMPBELL (ASCAP)

VIOLIN I

Christ Arose (Lo in the Grave He Lay)

CHRIST AROSE
Robert Lowery
Arr. KRISTIN CAMPBELL (ASCAP)

VIOLIN II

Christ Arose (Lo in the Grave He Lay)

CHRIST AROSE
Robert Lowery
Arr. KRISTIN CAMPBELL (ASCAP)

VIOLIN I

Like A River Glorious

WYE VALLEY
James Mountain
Arr. KRISTIN CAMPBELL (ASCAP)

VIOLIN II

Like A River Glorious

WYE VALLEY
James Mountain
Arr. KRISTIN CAMPBELL (ASCAP)

Rock of Ages

VIOLIN I

TOPLADY
Thomas Hastings
Arr. KRISTIN CAMPBELL (ASCAP)

VIOLIN II

Rock of Ages

TOPLADY
Thomas Hastings
Arr. KRISTIN CAMPBELL (ASCAP)

VIOLIN I

Guide Me O Thou Great Jehovah
Apples in Winter (Jig)

CWM RHONDDA
John Hughes
Arr. KRISTIN CAMPBELL (ASCAP)

GUIDE ME O THOU GREAT JEHOVAH - VIOLIN 1 - p. 2

VIOLIN II

Guide Me O Thou Great Jehovah

Apples in Winter (Jig)

CWM RHONDDA
John Hughes
Arr. KRISTIN CAMPBELL (ASCAP)

GUIDE ME O THOU GREAT JEHOVAH - VIOLIN II - p. 2

Hark the Herald Angels Sing

MENDELSSOHN
Felix Mendelssohn
Arr. KRISTIN CAMPBELL (ASCAP)

* 8va optional

VIOLIN II

Hark the Herald Angels Sing

MENDELSSOHN
Felix Mendelssohn
Arr. KRISTIN CAMPBELL (ASCAP)

* 8va optional

VIOLIN I

The Love of God

LOVE OF GOD
F. M. Lehman
Arr. KRISTIN CAMPBELL (ASCAP)

VIOLIN II

The Love of God

LOVE OF GOD
F. M. Lehman
Arr. KRISTIN CAMPBELL (ASCAP)

Calmly (♩ = 80)

VIOLIN I

Sleepers Awake

WACHET AUF
J.S. Bach
Arr. KRISTIN CAMPBELL (ASCAP)

SLEEPERS AWAKE - VIOLIN I - p. 2

Sleepers Awake

WACHET AUF
J.S. Bach
Arr. KRISTIN CAMPBELL (ASCAP)

SLEEPERS AWAKE - VIOLIN II - p. 2

Index

www.ingramcontent.com/pod-product-compliance
Lightning Source LLC
Chambersburg PA
CBHW081006120626
46546CB00010B/3040